THE NEW
MOON
HERBERT S. ZIM

illustrated with photographs
William Morrow and Company
New York 1980

Library of Congress Cataloging in Publication Data

Zim, Herbert Spencer, 1909-
  The new Moon.

  Summary: Presents information obtained from manned and unmanned lunar probes about the surface, atmosphere, and interior of the moon.
  1. Moon—Juvenile literature. [1. Moon] I. Title.
QB582.Z55   599'.99'1   79-21896
ISBN 0-688-22219-6   ISBN 0-688-32219-0 lib. bdg.

The author gratefully acknowledges the help of Dr. Bevan M. French and Mary Hill French for reading the text of this book and commenting on it. In addition to the help from Dr. French, he wishes to thank all the others on the National Aeronautics and Space Administration staff who have provided photographs and additional material.

All photographs courtesy of the National Aeronautics and Space Administration except for: page 24, right, Harold E. Edgerton, *Moments of Vision*, The MIT Press; pages 27, 38, Lick Observatory; page 32, National Park Service, U.S. Department of the Interior.

Metric measure, now used the world over, is also used in this book. Lengths and distances are based on the meter (m); 100 centimeters (cm) make one meter and 1000 meters make one kilometer (km). Weights are in kilograms (kg), and temperatures are in degrees Celsius (°C). A meter is just under 40 inches, a kilometer is 0.6 miles, a kilogram equals 2.2 pounds, and 100 degrees Celsius is the same as 212 degrees Fahrenheit.

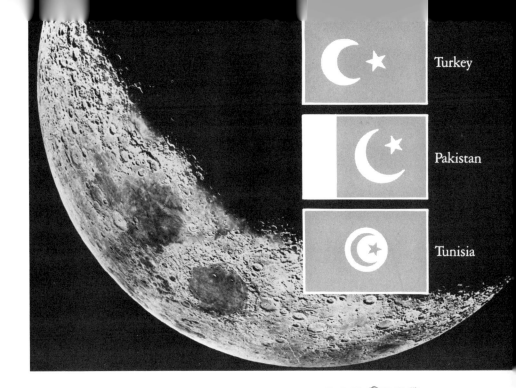

Turkey

Pakistan

Tunisia

2098862

Thirteen times a year, as you look westward just after sunset, the soft, upturned, thin crescent of the new moon catches your eye. Its delicate beauty is enjoyed today as it has been for thousands of years. Everyone knows the new moon. On their flags, countries like Turkey, Pakistan, and Tunisia show the new moon at the rare time when it seems to be close to Venus, the evening star.

The new moon, of course, is not really new. In fact, Luna, as it is properly called by scientists, has changed far less than planet Earth during the past two or three billion years. But since Luna orbits the Earth, our view of it changes daily. So, for centuries, people have thought of the moon as new when they watch it reappear as a thin crescent every twenty-eight days.

Our moon, the Earth's only natural satellite, is the best-known object in the night sky. The earliest people knew it and wondered about its changing shape. Knowledge of Luna and its movements grew with time. From about 5000 to 200 B.C., the Greeks and others observed it closely and plotted its changes.

During the next thousand years or so, Luna was neglected. Many people thought of the moon as an abode of spirits. They believed its changing phases controlled the growth of crops

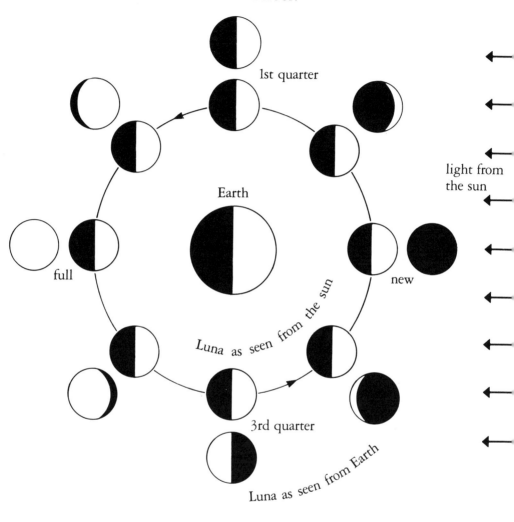

and even the daily lives of men and women. The
full moon was said to cause insanity, and men-
tally ill people were often called "lunatics."

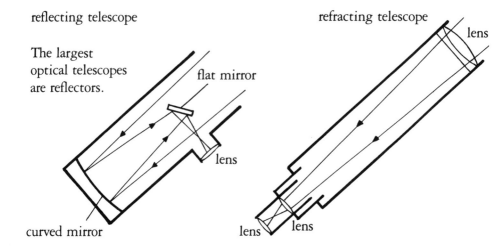

reflecting telescope

refracting telescope

The largest optical telescopes are reflectors.

flat mirror

lens

lens

lens

lens

curved mirror

    In the early 1600s, a new, clearer view of Luna became possible with that simple but magnificent invention, the telescope. Galileo built one in 1609 and was soon studying the heavens with it. From then on, astronomers, scientists who study the heavens, had a new moon to study— one brought much closer to Earth by the use of lenses or mirrors. Moon watchers could now see lunar mountains, craters, and huge dark "seas" known as maria.

    For the next 300 years our view of Luna did not change greatly. Larger telescopes, with cameras attached, showed more and more detail. Yet there was much that could not be seen or studied a quarter of a million miles away. In the 1960s and 1970s, we got another new and startling look at our moon.

This era started with Sputnik I, the Russian space satellite, launched in 1957. Soon American and Russian probes were on their way to Luna. In 1959, the first crude pictures of the unknown, far side of the moon were relayed back to Earth. Men who circled or landed on Luna

A very early lunar picture taken in 1966 by Surveyor 1, an unmanned vehicle that landed safely on Luna and sent back photographs of small rocks. This particular rock is 6 inches high and 12 inches long.

later came back with photographs, measurements, and specimens of moon rocks. These
data gave, at last, a detailed picture of what
Luna was really like.

Until this time, the moon had been studied
mainly by astronomers. Now geologists, who
are concerned with rocks, and other kinds of
scientists began studying it too. Manned and
unmanned vehicles delivered 382 kilograms of
lunar rock back to Earth. Scientists all over the
world analyzed and studied them, learning how
and when they were formed.

Geologists examine small lunar samples brought back by Apollo 11.

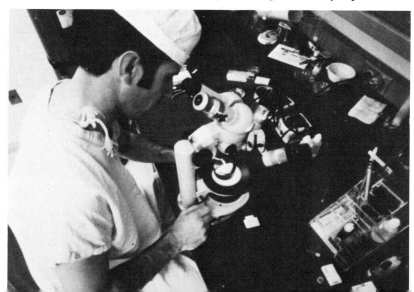

MOST COMMON ELEMENTS
on Earth and Luna, free or combined
(approximate amounts from crust)

Element	Earth	Luna	Element	Earth	Luna
Oxygen	46%	42%	Calcium	4%	4%
Silicon	28	21	Sodium	3	.01
Aluminum	8	4	Potassium	3	.08
Iron	5	8	Magnesium	2	19

On Luna, titanium, chromium, and manganese are more common than sodium and potassium, but still less than 1%.

A hundred or so elements make up the universe. The atoms of each have different weights and properties. Of these elements, hydrogen and helium are the lightest and most common. Both are gases. But the inner planets and other smaller bodies in the solar system are not typical of the rest of the universe. The light elements are lacking on them, and on Luna too. On planet Earth much of its small amount of hydrogen is combined with oxygen, forming the water that makes our oceans and rivers.

On both Earth and Luna, chemical elements rarely exist independently. Two, three, or more of them are usually joined together in definite chemical patterns. The compounds thus formed look and act quite differently from the elements of which they are made. Natural solid compounds (and a few elements) found in the crust of Earth and Luna are called "minerals." Minerals, in turn, make up rocks.

Sodium, a soft, silvery, dangerous metal, and chlorine, a greenish, poisonous gas, join to make sodium chloride, a white compound you know and use as table salt.

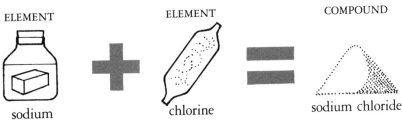

ELEMENT   ELEMENT   COMPOUND

sodium   chlorine   sodium chloride

When sodium chloride occurs naturally in the crust of the Earth it becomes halite, a mineral that forms cubic crystals.

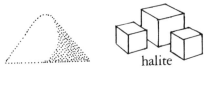

halite

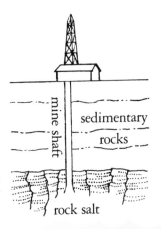

mine shaft

sedimentary rocks

Large beds of halite are also a rock—rock salt.

rock salt

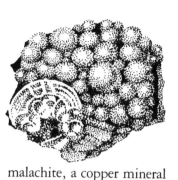

malachite, a copper mineral

siderite, an iron mineral

uranophane, a uranium mineral

In each of these minerals a metal is combined with elements from water or air.

Over two thousand kinds of minerals have been found on Earth. On Luna, which has been explored in a very limited way, only about one hundred have been discovered, and nearly all of them are minerals known on Earth also. This lesser amount is due to the lack of water, gases, and many light elements on Luna. Thus, scientists do not expect to find many new lunar minerals in the future.

The most common minerals on both Earth and Luna are formed from the most common elements. At or near the surface, these minerals are silicates, containing the elements silicon and oxygen plus one or more others. Examples are the feldspars, pyroxenes, and olivine. Earth is richer in micas, amphiboles, and the common mineral quartz. Lunar rocks contain more titanium than those on Earth. Two interesting titanium minerals are known only on Luna.

MINERALS ABUNDANT ON BOTH EARTH AND LUNA

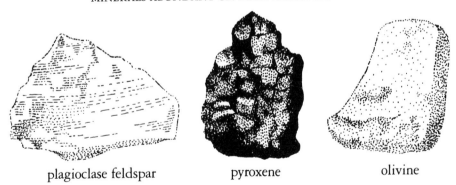

plagioclase feldspar   pyroxene   olivine

These rock-forming minerals are found in igneous rocks. Quartz is another such mineral, but it is much more common on Earth than on Luna.

Troctolite, a very old crystalline lunar rock, formed below the surface but was broken and thrown out by impacts. The darker areas are olivine, the lighter ones, feldspar. Both minerals are common on Earth.

The common rocks on planet Earth are those formed through the action of water and air. None of this type is found on Luna, where practically all rocks are igneous. That is, the rocks were once molten and have cooled. Their minerals form masses of interlocked crystals or glass. They include lavas and the crystalline rocks of the lunar highlands.

The best-known lunar rock, of those collected by the astronauts, is lunar basalt, a lava. It is not the most common rock on our moon, but it is the most familiar since it is very much like basalt found here on Earth. The differences are small. The minerals in lunar basalt, for example, are like those in Earth basalts, but they do not appear in exactly the same amounts. Lunar basalts also seem to melt and flow more easily than ours.

So important are lunar basalts that experts have carefully studied all that have been brought back. They find three types. Those from the maria, or lunar seas, usually contain more iron

Basalts as shown here filled many lunar craters and basins. These dark rocks, rich in titanium, formed and spread about 3.7 billion years ago.

and less aluminum. Those found in the high-lands tend to have more aluminum and calcium, but less iron and magnesium. Finally, an un-usual group called KREEP basalts contain more potassium (chemical abbreviation K), rare earth elements (abbreviated REE), and more phos-phorus (abbreviated P). KREEP basalts also con-tain traces of radioactive elements, used in determining the rock's age. They and all the other lunar rocks were formed at high tempera-tures, about 1000 to 1500 degrees Celsius.

Basalts with gas bubbles were more common as the lava flows died out. At this time (about 3.3 billion years ago) Luna was cooling off.

The top of this breccia is basalt, showing that it is younger than the maria lavas. The white fragments are much older crystalline rocks.

Several kinds of crystalline rocks probably covered the moon at one time. As thousands upon thousands of meteors crashed into Luna they were broken into rock fragments, mostly three to four billion years ago. The impact of these collisions released tremendous energy that shattered, altered, and even melted the rocks of which the moon was formed. These fragments, cemented by the heat and pressure, became rocks that are known as breccias.

Some of the breccias on Luna were formed and re-formed by several explosive impacts. Only small bits of the original igneous rocks remain in them. Yet scientists are able to study these bits to learn what the older rocks were like. Eight kinds of breccias have been classified, depending on the temperature that the meteor collision generated. Minerals in some have developed new crystals. The heat, ranging from about 600 to 1200 degrees Celsius, has also made several kinds of natural glass.

This highland breccia has a long history. Ancient regolith and rock were fused, and more recently a meteor impact added melted black glass.

Rock fragments that were not cemented into breccias still cover much of the lunar surface in a thick, loose layer. Most of this layer is a fine, gray dust, but it also includes sand, pebbles, and even rocks and boulders. From 10 to 85 percent of the fine material is made up of very tiny balls of glass, formed by impact heat and pressure. All this loose material is called "regolith," or "lunar soil." It covers Luna like soil on Earth, but often in a much thicker layer that may be one to one and a half kilometers deep.

On Earth, soil is formed from solid rocks by the action of rain, frost, ice, wind, plants, and animals. Lunar regolith is made by collisions and explosions. Soil usually contains plant ma-

Tiny glass balls are found in the regolith. (enlarged)

Astronaut collecting rock material from the soft, powdery regolith.

terial and other traces of life. On lifeless Luna, this important ingredient is missing. But when seeds were planted in samples of regolith brought back to laboratories on Earth, they grew quite well.

The lunar rocks form the moon's surface structures, the equivalent of the Earth's hills, valleys, cliffs, canyons, and peaks. But the forces that created these features on Luna, while partly similar, are generally quite different from those on Earth.

Largest and oldest lunar structures are the great ringed basins. These basins mark the impact of very large meteors, comets, or possibly still larger asteroids or planetoids. Most ringed basins are overlapped by craters, large and small, produced by other common lunar impacts. A number have been filled, at least in part, by lava flows. Forty-three such large ringed basins have been mapped. More may be hidden by the scars of younger craters.

One basin called Imbrium is about the size of Texas. No signs of collision impacts this large have been found on Earth, though they may have existed very long ago. Another lunar basin may be 2000 kilometers in diameter and about 8 kilometers deep. Experts think that these large basins may have been blasted 250 to 700 kilometers deep, but they were immediately filled, or nearly so, by the broken rock and debris.

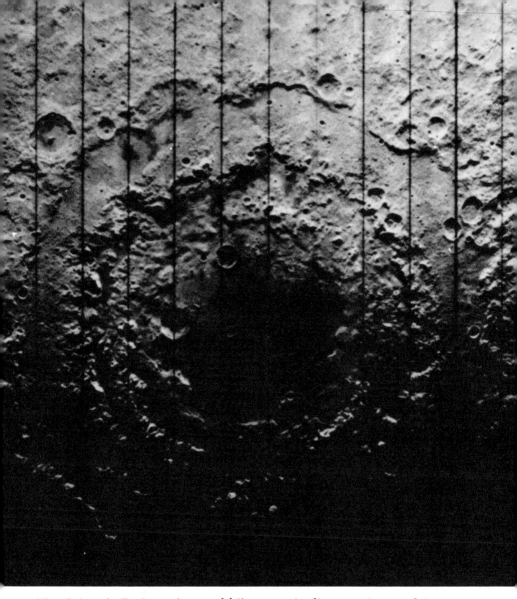

The Orientale Basin, a thousand kilometers in diameter, is one of the larger ringed basins. Just on the edge of the visible side of Luna, it cannot be seen completely. Some of the basin is filled with basalt. An inner ring of mountains forms another circle 640 kilometers across. The basin seems to be one of the youngest of its kind.

The lunar craters, which cover most of the surface of the moon, are more familiar structures. The largest are easily seen from Earth with a small telescope. Astronomers noted them some 300 years ago and argued about them for many years. One group held that they were great volcanoes like those found around the Pacific Ocean basin. More recently, because of detailed lunar observations, they have been recognized as impact craters. This conclusion was supported by evidence from experimental craters made here in the United States by underground nuclear test explosions.

Large lunar craters are from one to one hundred kilometers in diameter, but a few have measured about twice as large, with depths of two to five kilometers. Most are younger than the ringed basins, a few being only about 100 million years old.

At 100 million years of age, Tycho is the youngest major ray crater on Luna. It is designated "major" because of its size—87 kilometers in diameter and 4.3 kilometers in depth. It is called a "ray crater" because the great impact scattered debris in rays going out from the crater for hundreds of kilometers. The photograph, taken from a lunar orbiter, shows the strong shadows when the sun is low. In this picture the sunlight is coming from the right.

Left: Crater Taruntius, a large (56 kilometers in diameter) but shallow crater with a central peak.
Right: Impact of falling drop of milk (caught by high-speed camera) forms the same pattern as meteors did on Luna.

Some of the large craters have a sharp peak at their center. Studies of lunar photographs and those of simple impact experiments show how such peaks form. Very high-speed photography of a falling drop of milk catches it throwing up such a central peak for a tiny fraction of a second during impact. Some of the great ringed basins have a similar inner ring of sharp peaks.

Smaller craters, most less than one kilometer in diameter, appear everywhere. Literally millions of them spot the lunar surface. Most were caused by the direct impact of small meteors.

Some were formed by the debris thrown out of large craters made by larger impacts, which scattered rock in all directions.

Craters only a few meters across do not penetrate the lunar surface deeply. Hence, they have formed largely in the regolith, breaking this loose surface material into finer and finer pieces. Old regolith often becomes compacted into breccia. The action of these small craters, breaking, mixing, and packing the regolith, had much to do with the making of this widespread rock.

Two medium (10 kilometers in diameter) and many small craters near crater Taruntius.

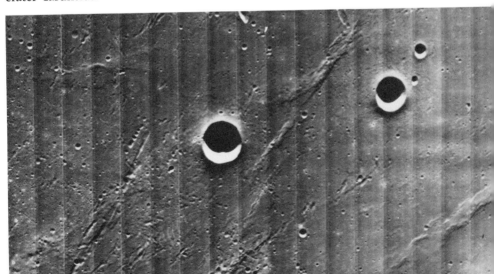

Meteors of noticeable size, from 100 grams to 1000 kilograms in weight, still strike Luna at a rate of about 70 to 150 per year. This rate is probably lower than it was in the distant past and is based on limited estimates that may change as new impacts are recorded.

Yet Luna did not have a great flood of meteors long ago. The very large collisions—the kind that formed the ringed basins—probably occurred only about once in a hundred million years. Smaller impacts were much more common, but they too spread over millions of years.

The most recent large impacts on Luna happened 100 million to 900 million years ago. They left a special record of large "young" craters. Outstanding are three that range from 32 to 90 kilometers in diameter and are 3 to 4 kilometers deep. All are marked by fresh, well-preserved debris thrown out by the impact. This

debris has fallen on top of lava flows and regolith, forming huge rays of rock fragments extending out from the craters for distances of
1000 kilometers or more. Rays from the crater
Tycho are so distinct that you can see them when
the moon is full, even without a telescope. The
two other famous "young" craters are Kepler
and Copernicus.

Full moon showing Kepler, Copernicus, and Tycho with its bright rays
extending thousands of kilometers.

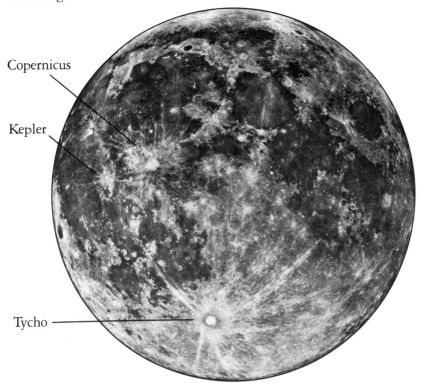

Copernicus

Kepler

Tycho

By far the most common structures on Luna are the smallest. They are microcraters that measure from .001 of a centimeter to 1 centimeter in diameter. They go unnoticed, for most are too small to see without a microscope. But when they are enlarged and examined, they appear to be a most unusual lunar feature. Caused by high-speed micrometeors, they are produced be-

Tip of a small glass-coated stone on Luna, its surface pitted by micro-impacts. (enlarged)

cause Luna has no protecting atmosphere. On Earth such tiny meteors leave no trace, for they never reach the surface with any energy. On Luna they strike with full speed. The micro impacts on Luna show most clearly on the minute glass spheres in the regolith. Every square centimeter of the lunar surface has received many such micro impacts.

A clump of fine regolith bonded and melted together by high speed micro-meteor impacts to form a glassy particle. (enlarged)

These lunar surface features, large and small, are due to impacts of material from space. Other structures may have different causes. The large lava flows of the maria are examples. The heat of great meteor impacts may have melted rock deep in the lunar crust. If so, this melted rock later came to the surface as basalt lava flows. But other sources of this internal heat are possible. It may come from uranium and other radioactive minerals as heat still comes from deep within the Earth.

Craters on the far side of Luna near the south pole. Those to the left are filled with basalt. Those to the right are not.

An unusual lunar feature—a long (120 kilometers) narrow, basalt-filled valley in a straight line. It was discovered near Mare Imbrium.

The fact remains that great and small basalt flows have spread over Luna for a long period of time. Some extend from 400 to 1000 kilometers and have covered areas larger than the great basalt flows along the Columbia River in Washington. Those on Luna may also be much thicker.

Younger lunar basalt flows show volcanic details that are also seen here on Earth. Canyons, or rilles, several kilometers wide and hundreds long, have been noted. Narrow valleys, or channels, tubes, ridges, and wrinkles, appear in photographs of lunar lava, too.

Despite all the lava flows on Luna, there are very few volcanoes, especially the high, conical ones formed of light lavas, cinders, and ash. Some low, rounded mounds, where the dark, liquid lava has spread widely, seem to be basalt volcanoes, but they never formed a sharp volcanic peak. Other possible volcanoes look as if they have caved in at the top, forming basins, or calderas, like Crater Lake in Oregon. Geologists wish that the true volcanoes on Luna had been explored more closely.

The caldera, or basin, atop a huge volcano in Oregon has filled with water to become Crater Lake. There may be calderas on Luna, but the basins are all dry.

A highland rock, formed over 4 billion years ago, was cut and polished into a thin section. The microscope shows it to be mainly the mineral feldspar. The black grains are pyroxene. (enlarged)

The highlands of Luna reveal mountains, hills, cliffs, ridges, peaks, and valleys like those on Earth. Highlands are the oldest part of the lunar surface, but their pattern is broken by craters, which are more numerous here. Astronauts have not obtained enough highland rocks for scientists to piece together their complex history. When they are available, the story of these oldest rocks may be completed.

The great mystery of Luna used to be the nature of the far side. Since Luna turns only once on its axis as it revolves once around Earth, people could only see the near side of Luna. Now space vehicles have circled Luna, and they have brought back thousands of photographs of the far side. Today the mystery is gone.

This distant photograph of Luna shows most of its far side.

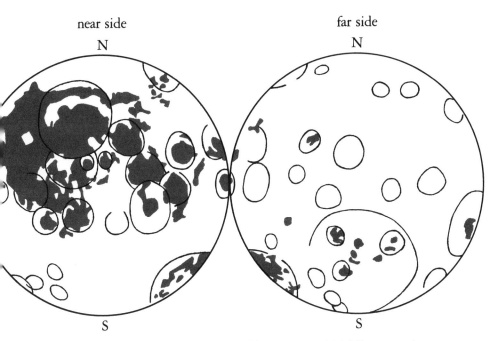

Black boundaries are those of large ringed basins (over 220 kilometers in diameter). Gray areas are basalt lava flows.

Scientists find that the far side of Luna is not very different from the familiar near side. The flows of smooth, dark basalt are much more limited. The great ringed basins are more common and are better preserved. Basins on the near side usually contain lava flows; those on the far side do not. Parts of the far side have many more craters than the side we see.

The surface of Luna is nothing but rock. Seventy percent of the Earth's surface is covered by oceans. Much of the rest is hidden under lakes, swamps, farms, forests, and cities. In addition, the Earth is wrapped like a package in a layer of air. This atmosphere is over a trillion times as dense as that of Luna.

Careful tests find only the barest trace of lunar atmosphere. On Earth, the molecules of nitrogen and oxygen that make up most of the air are so closely packed that they are constantly colliding—and at a tremendous rate. On Luna, the air molecules are so few and far apart they rarely, if ever, collide. They are molecules of hydrogen, helium, neon, and argon, and a few of oxygen and carbon dioxide. There is no water at all.

Air molecules on Earth constantly collide.

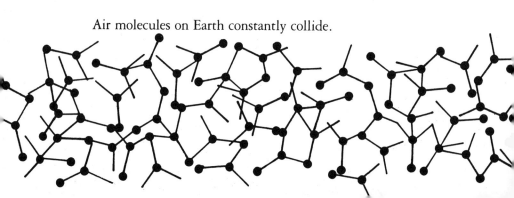

COMPARISON OF LUNAR AND EARTH ATMOSPHERES

Luna	Earth
about 200,000 molecules of gas per c.c. at surface; probably no atmosphere at all	about 25,000,000,000,000,000,000 molecules of gas per c.c. at surface, 100,000,000,000,000 times as many as on Luna
marked changes between day and night	composition at surface stable and unchanging
traces of hydrogen, helium, neon, argon, oxygen, carbon dioxide	78% nitrogen, 21% oxygen, 1% argon; traces of helium, methane, krypton, xenon, ozone, carbon dioxide plus water

The lack of an atmosphere makes Luna different. No wind, rain, ice, or chemical change alters the surface rock. It remains as it once was billions of years ago. On Earth, the rocks are slowly but constantly changing, even those that are very deeply buried. But while the surface rocks on Luna remain unchanged, they are altered in very slight but unusual and important

Air molecules on Luna rarely collide.

ways. These changes are due to intense flows of energy that mark the central part of our solar system, where Luna and Earth are located.

Into our area come rays and particles from far outer space that may have had their start at the very origin of the universe itself. These cosmic rays have very high energy and reach us from far outside our solar system.

From the sun itself come other particles and rays, usually related to the great hydrogen explosions called "solar flares." These outbursts are

Solar flares streak out from the sun for thousands of miles.

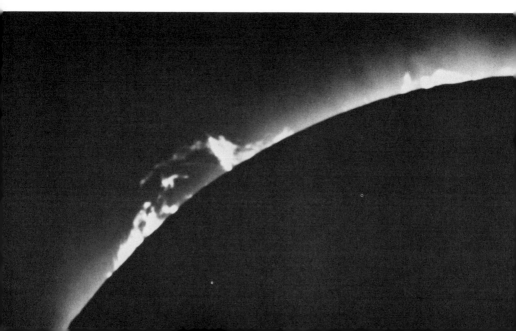

at a lower energy level than cosmic rays. Another kind of radiation, at a still lower energy level, also comes from the sun. It is mainly particles of charged hydrogen, expelled from the sun at speeds of 300 to 500 kilometers per second—a flow of radiation called the "solar wind."

On planet Earth, these space radiations are difficult and often impossible to detect, measure, and study. The Earth's magnetic field diverts some of them. The dense atmosphere, especially its upper layers, absorbs a good deal. Radiation reaching the ocean is lost. There is very little chance that any record of radiation is left on the surface rocks. They are constantly being altered as they are worn away by wind, ice, and water.

Complex foil strips set up by astronauts have recorded the impacts of solar-wind particles on Luna

On Luna, with no atmosphere to shield it from radiation, the record is much clearer. New and delicate techniques reveal the tracks of atomic particles in lunar rocks. Six Apollo missions conducted solar-wind experiments, trapping the solar radiation on sheets of aluminum foil. Cores of material were dug from the regolith to get undisturbed samples of rock. These bits of fresh material were treated to reveal particle tracks.

Core samples dug by Apollo 12 crew. This fine regolith contained materials that had not been exposed to solar wind and other radiation recently.

By heating samples of lunar rock, gases are driven off and collected. Some of these gases may be due to radiation or to radioactivity.

Thus, data on solar wind and solar flares gathered on Luna have provided scientists with new information on solar radiation. Apparently the energy flow from our sun has not changed much for a billion years or so. Other radiation records in lunar rocks help geologists understand their age and history.

Many early students of the heavens believed that Luna was the home of strange creatures. But as scientists learned that Luna had neither air nor water, they doubted more and more that life could exist on it. Still, the idea was never completely dropped. Some thought that microscopic life might survive on Luna. Others wondered if moon fossils would show that life did exist there long ago.

The chance to answer the question about life

While no life was found on Luna, lunar soil was tested to see its effects on plants.

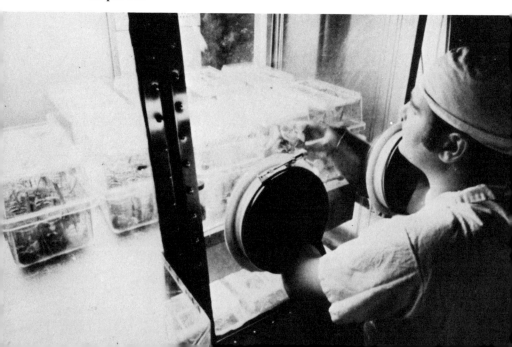

definitely came when moon rocks were brought back to Earth. Astronauts saw no life on Luna, but some might exist in the specimens they collected. These specimens were completely protected from contact with air or any life on Earth. Some 3000 laboratory tests, under many different conditions, were made. No sign of lunar life ever appeared. Detailed studies failed to turn up any fossils or other clues to extinct lunar life.

Several kinds of plants grew well in contact with lunar soil or regolith.

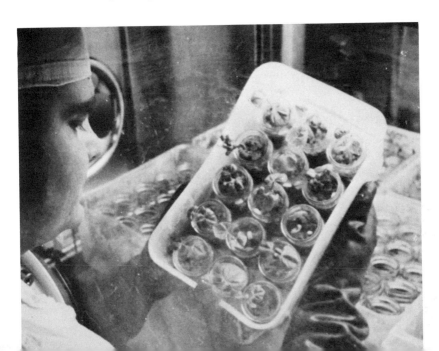

Small amounts of carbon (an element closely linked to life on Earth) have been found on Luna. These very small traces are about the same as those found in many stony meteors—an amount far too small to indicate life. This faint trace of carbon probably came to Luna in radiation from the sun or in stony meteors.

All of the lunar rock collected by astronauts was taken from the surface or from shallow holes. But the surface itself is a mixed jumble of rock fragments, some blasted out from deep

Many surface rocks were collected on Luna, but they do not tell much of the moon's deep interior.

craters. These pieces offer some clues about deeper rocks. Yet we still have very little direct knowledge of the lunar interior. Scientists anxious to learn more about the interior of Luna will have to study the lunar rocks further. One way is to find out how those deep inside Luna react to waves or vibrations passing through them.

On Earth, huge plates of rock move past or over each other. When they do, they set up the waves, or tremors, known as an earthquake. Delicate devices record these tremors and the

Some of Earth's great crustal plates. Earthquakes are common along the plate boundaries.

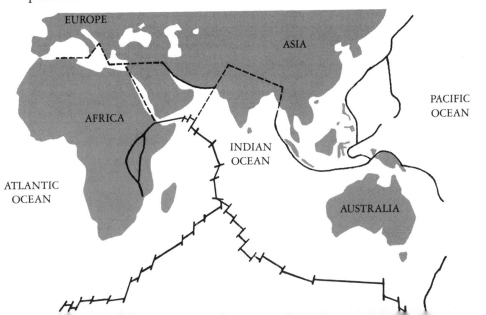

speed at which they travel. This information gives clues to materials and conditions deep inside the Earth.

Tremors occur on Luna also, but moonquakes are not common. There are less than about 3000 of them a year, compared to perhaps 3000 a day on Earth. All the tremors on Luna and nearly all on Earth are so mild they cannot be felt. To get more information, astronauts set off small underground explosions that made mild tremors. Earth geologists do the same thing when search-

Apollo 14 astronauts used a seismograph wrapped in a thermal blanket to measure moonquakes and to determine the lunar interior from the speed of waves going through it.

ing for oil deposits. Luckily, a fair-sized meteor struck the far side of Luna in 1972, causing strong moon tremors that were easily measured.

From these limited data comes the first picture of the lunar interior. It starts with a crust about 60 kilometers thick. This crust includes a kilometer or more of regolith, various breccias, and flows of basalt. Deeper into the crust (25-60 kilometers), the rock pressure wipes out all cracks once formed by impacts, making the rocky material solid.

On July 17, 1972, all the seismographs on Luna recorded a major moonquake, probably due to the impact of a large meteor on the far side. The differences in the seismograph recordings, one of which is shown below, gave the best clues on the lunar interior.

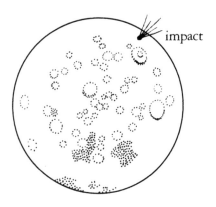

impact

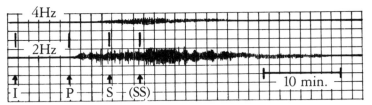

48

Beneath this crust is a layer, extending inward another 1000 kilometers or so, composed mainly of solid rocks. They are probably like the heavier igneous rocks of the Earth. Near the bottom of this denser mantle region is where the deep moonquakes occur.

The interior of Luna is known mainly from the way moonquake waves travel through it. The surface crust is thicker than that of Earth. The mantle beneath is solid rock, which merges into a central core. This core may be partly melted and seems to be of iron or iron combined with sulfur.

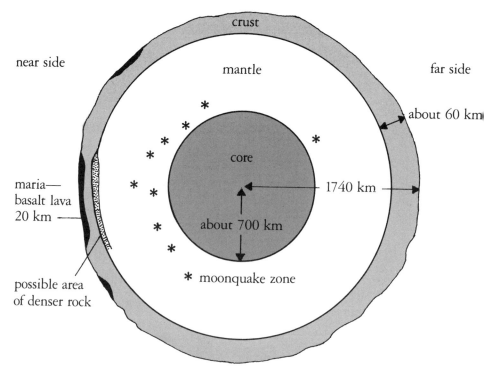

Finally, the lunar core extends inward another 700 kilometers to the very center of Luna. It is a region about which little is known. The core may be solid, partly molten, or perhaps both. After the large meteor struck the far side of Luna in 1972, certain expected moonquake waves did not appear. This type of wave form is absorbed by liquids, so possibly Luna has a molten zone deep within. The different densities of lunar rocks suggest that the core is iron or iron-sulphur. This core may be surrounded by the molten, or fluid, zone. One thing is certain—more data on Luna's interior are needed.

Two of the instruments used on Luna.
The magnetometer (*left*) measures the very weak magnetism.
The gravimeter (*right*) measures very small changes in gravity.

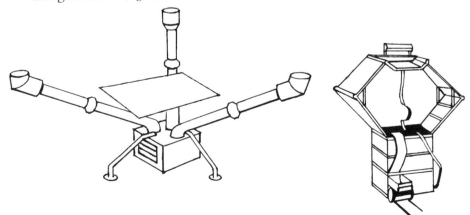

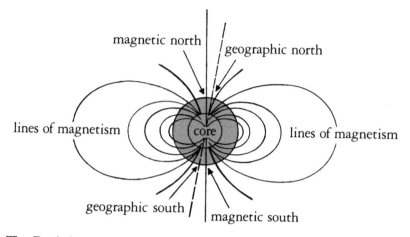

The Earth has a magnetic field that extends far out into space. The magnetic poles are about 2000 kilometers away from the north and south geographic poles.

The limited iron in Luna's core or the lack of it helps explain why there is almost no magnetism on the moon. Our Earth is a huge magnet with north and south magnetic poles. Thus, the compass can be used to find direction or to travel along a desired route. Why the Earth is a magnet is related to its fluid iron core and to the Earth's rotation, which makes it act like a gigantic, low-powered electric dynamo.

Luna barely has a magnetic field at all, as Apollo measurements clearly show. In a few local areas, there is a bit of lunar magnetism. On the average, however, it is less than half of 1 percent of Earth's. This tiny bit seems to be what is called "fossil magnetism," which has remained in lunar rock for between three to four billion years. Then the interior of Luna may have been hotter, and if so, the iron in its core was completely melted. Under such conditions, magnetism might have been generated just as it is on Earth. Since that time Luna's interior has not been hot enough to melt iron completely, so no source of magnetism now exists—or so we think.

These submicroscopic iron crystals were formed in the heat of impact, a billion years or more after the core of Luna had formed.

The elements, minerals, rocks, and structures on and in Luna fit into a continuing story that is partly like, but mainly different, from Earth's. Most similar is the very beginning, which for both Luna and Earth is still veiled in mystery. As best we know, some five billion years ago or more, this part of the universe was a whirling disc of hot gases that were drawn tighter and tighter by gravity and other forces. Most of this great disc pulled together and formed our sun. Other smaller areas of dust and gases condensed and formed planets and satellites. Scientists think that this birth of the solar system happened about four and a half billion years ago.

At this stage and for the next half a billion years or more, all parts of the solar system were pelted by meteors and other space debris as the system formed. The collisions with larger bodies also added to and changed the surface of Luna, Earth, and other planets. Then, on Luna, began a period of another billion years, marked by great floods of basalt lava that spread, filling the ringed basins and many large craters.

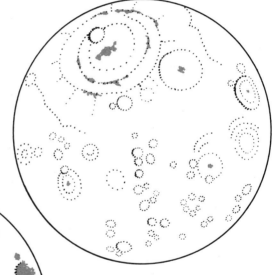

Nearly four billion years ago the moon's surface pattern was already set. Scars from large and small impacts covered the entire surface.

Just over half a billion years later most of the large basins were flooded by maria basalts. New large craters had formed. Luna has changed very little in the past three billion years.

Similar events probably took place on Earth, but the action of water, air, and interior movements over several billion years have destroyed the evidence here. On Luna, free from surface changes caused by water or air, the rocks and their structures have remained almost exactly as they were three billion years ago. Some lava flows have spread since, and even today Luna shows some slight traces of activity. These movements are Lunar Transient Phenomena (LTP), which are now recorded and studied. They include light or glowing areas, haze, and clouds, especially near a few craters.

Earth, too, has transient phenomena, and they are on a far greater scale than Luna's. Storms, lightning, floods, earthquakes, and forest fires are examples of them.

This general story of the birth and growth of the solar system, Earth, and Luna is widely accepted. Scientists are less sure about the details and are more likely to argue about them. The origin of Luna is a good example. One theory was that Luna is not a moon at all, but another smaller planet captured by Earth soon after the solar system was formed. Another group thought that Luna was formed from materials thrown off from Earth when it was hotter and spinning faster. A third idea was that Luna and the Earth were twin planets, formed at the same time and revolving around each other ever since.

We know much less about how Luna began than about how it developed. All the theories below seem possible.

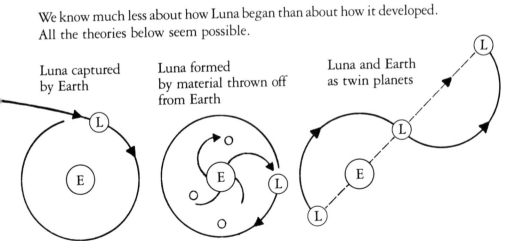

Luna captured by Earth

Luna formed by material thrown off from Earth

Luna and Earth as twin planets

Some facts support each of these ideas; other facts show that each may be impossible. With more time, more facts, and further study, an acceptable idea of the origin of Luna may appear. Until that time a compromise has been suggested.

Possibly the very early stages of the solar system were marked by smaller lumps of matter in space being pulled toward larger ones by gravity. When close enough, these lumps moved into orbit around their captor. Those that came near to Earth and were captured may have formed a ring of mixed rocky materials around our planet. These circling bits and pieces continued to collide and merge with larger ones. Luna may be the result of thousands upon thousands of collisions, which built our moon up to its present size.

Whatever its origin, Luna has now been ex-

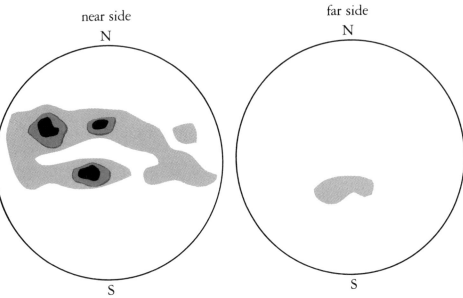

near side   far side
N   N

S   S

Areas on Luna richer in radioactive rocks. The darker the color the more the radiation. Not all the lunar surface has been checked in this research.

plored, though on a very limited scale. The many observations of astronauts on Luna and from orbiting vehicles have been extended by their experiments. Magnetism, radioactivity, and the solar wind have been studied. Slight variations in the speed of orbiting spacecraft, due to slight changes in the gravity pull of Luna, have led to the discovery of local areas of denser lunar rocks. These areas of mass concentration

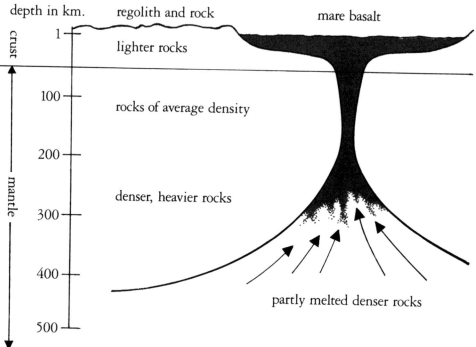

depth in km.   regolith and rock   mare basalt

crust

1 — lighter rocks

mantle

100 — rocks of average density

200 —

denser, heavier rocks

300 —

400 —

partly melted denser rocks

500 —

Mascons occur with lava-filled basins. The density of rocks beneath them increases from depths of 100 to over 400 kilometers. Here the pressure on partly melted rocks increases the density of the area.

are called "mascons." Using accurate photographs, scientists have now mapped Luna as well as some of the Earth is mapped.

Opposite: From thousands of lunar photographs, 127 special ones taken from lunar orbiter IV were selected and enlarged to the same scale. These pictures were assembled into a thirty-foot map of the near side of Luna, a remarkable job of mapping.

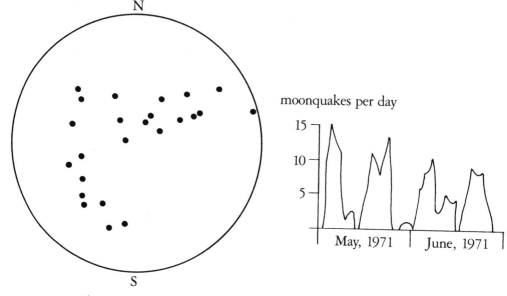

moonquakes per day

About 800 kilometers beneath each of these spots on Luna (near side) is the place where a moonquake originated. Moonquakes are very weak. Most occur when the moon is closest to Earth.

Automatic apparatus left behind on Luna gathered data and sent back reports for several years. One located and measured moonquakes, even minor ones. Its records show that moonquakes are more common twice a month at the times when Luna is nearest Earth in its orbit.

Perhaps no other scientific effort has equaled that of reaching, circling, and putting men on the moon. In terms of the number of experts involved, the cost, and the difficult problems that were solved, the effort was outstanding.

Those who knew very little about Luna thought that astronauts might find materials of great value there. Such people were disappointed. Lunar rocks do contain traces of gold, about as much as is in the water of our oceans. Astronomers, who had been studying Luna for the past century or so, had clear ideas as to what might be found. These ideas were confirmed by the landings. Scientists were quite sure Luna was lifeless. Now they are even more positive.

Apollo 15 landing module and lunar roving vehicle on Luna, July, 1971.

Besides confirming some ideas and setting aside some others, the trips to Luna had greater value. The dated rocks established a complete time scale for Luna's existence, which has increased our knowledge of the entire solar system. With Luna as the first step, space-vehicle exploration of Venus, Mars, Jupiter, and Saturn is under way. New data are already in. With clues from Luna, the early history of the Earth is being restudied. New evidence of ancient great impacts have been found on our planet.

Here, in Quebec, at Manicouagan, a great meteor or an asteroid may have formed this 66-kilometer crater some 22 million years ago. Most of the crater has worn away, but the changes in the melted and shattered rock are still clear.

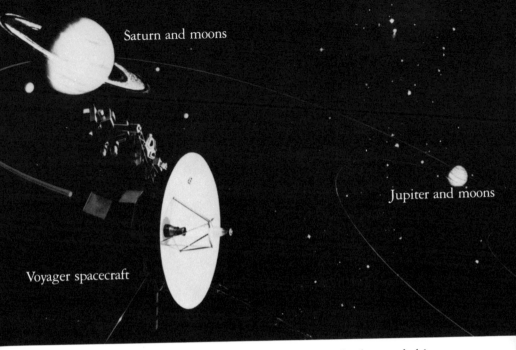

Saturn and moons

Jupiter and moons

Voyager spacecraft

Voyager space vehicles and others (unmanned) have sent back remarkable photographs of Venus, Mars, Jupiter, and Saturn. They greatly increase our knowledge of the solar system.

The moon voyages have given us answers to questions that have long puzzled scientists. Furthermore, the data from Apollo and the Voyager explorations have turned up new, better, and more penetrating questions. This is the way that science progresses—every discovery made shows how much more remains to be discovered. Who knows what still lies ahead?

INDEX *indicates illustration*